Badger Publishing Limited
Oldmedow Road,
Hardwick Industrial Estate,
King's Lynn PE30 4JJ
Telephone: 01438 791037

www.badgerlearning.co.uk

4 6 8 10 9 7 5 3

Hip Hop ISBN 978-1-78464-130-6

Text © Tim Collins 2015

Complete work © Badger Publishing Limited 2015

All rights reserved. No part of this publication may be reproduced, stored in any form or by any means mechanical, electronic, recording or otherwise without the prior permission of the publisher.

The right of Tim Collins to be identified as author of this work has been asserted by him in accordance with the Copyright, Designs and Patents Act 1988.

Publisher: Susan Ross
Senior Editor: Danny Pearson
Publishing Assistant: Claire Morgan
Designer: Cathryn Gilbert
Series Consultant: Dee Reid
Copyeditor: Cheryl Lanyon

Photos: Cover Image: © Carlos's Pemium Images/Alamy
Page 5: Greg Allen/REX
Page 6: Robin Anderson/REX
Page 7: Nigel Howard/Associated News/REX
Page 8: © Gijsbert Hanekroot/Alamy
Page 10: Ted Polhemus/PYMCA/REX
Page 11: Courtesy Everett Collection/REX
Page 12: © Granamour Weems Collection/Alamy
Page 13: Josh Cheuse/PYMCA /REX, SIPA PRESS/REX, Everett Collection/REX
Page 14: RL/KEYSTONE USA/REX
Page 15: REX
Page 18: PictureGroup/REX
Page 19: Clare Muller/PYMCA/REX
Page 20: Everett Collection/REX
Page 21: East News/REX
Page 22: © PYMCA/Alamy
Page 23: FOTOS INTERNATIONAL/REX, Action Press/REX
Page 25: © epa european pressphoto agency b.v./Alamy
Page 26: Sonny Meddle/REX
Page 27: Naki/PYMCA/REX
Page 28: Scott Aiken/REX
Page 29: Eye Candy/REX
Page 30: © incamerastock/Alamy

Attempts to contact all copyright holders have been made.
If any omitted would care to contact Badger Learning, we will be happy to make appropriate arrangements.

Contents

1. What is hip hop?   5
2. The roots of hip hop   8
3. The ages of rap   12
4. Is rap poetry?   16
5. Hip hop fashion   19
6. Hip hop around the world   26
7. How to become a rapper   29

Questions   31

Index   32

Vocabulary

accessory influence
acrobatic instrumental
encouraging revolution
fashionable simile

1. What is Hip Hop?

Hip hop began in New York in the 1970s. It was created by people who didn't have much money or power, but it went on to take over the world.

These days its influence can be seen everywhere, and rappers such as Jay Z, Dr. Dre and Eminem are global superstars.

But what exactly is hip hop and how did it begin?

Some people think rap and hip hop are the same thing but they are different. Hip hop is the movement that grew from 1970s New York. Rap was just one part of this.

You can see the impact of hip hop on fashion, advertising, design, television and film.

Some hip hop words have become words that everyone uses now: bling, diss and chill.

There are four traditional elements of hip hop:

- **Rapping** – saying words to a backing beat.

- **DJ-ing** – creating new music by mixing together records on turntables. The backing beat is usually made this way.

- **Breakdancing** – energetic dance that can include spinning and headstands.

- **Graffiti** – street art made with spray cans and marker pens.

2. The Roots of Hip Hop

The Bronx area of New York where hip hop began was a poor part of the city. But the young people who lived there wanted to create their own music and style.

WOW! facts

The term hip hop has been used for rap culture since the late 1970s, but it was first used in a 1671 play by the Duke of Buckingham. He used it to describe a hopping motion!

They held large outdoor events which were called block parties. They played music very loudly.

The DJs made the instrumental parts, or 'breaks', of popular songs longer. They used two copies of the same record and switched from one to the other to play the break over and over again. Street dancers loved this.

In 1977, DJ Kool Herc said:

> *"And when I extended the break, people were ecstatic, because that was the best part of the record to dance to, and they were trippin' off it."*

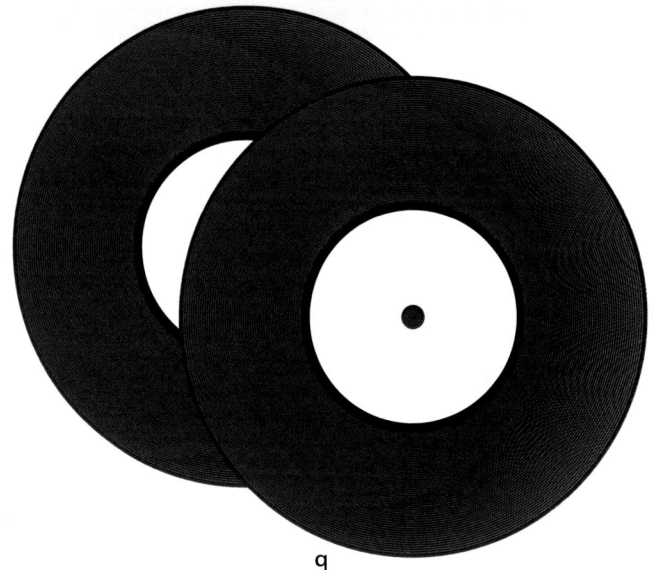

The longer breaks between the lyrics, or words, of the song meant street dancers could perform acrobatic moves such as spinning on their backs.

This became known as 'breakdancing'.

At the same time, people began to speak over the breaks. At first they copied a fast Jamaican tradition known as 'toasting'. But they soon developed a slower, more American style, which became rap.

Many of the important DJs from this era are still remembered today. They include Grandmaster Flash, Kool Herc and Afrika Bambaataa.

The young people who were better at art than music and dance joined in the hip hop revolution by becoming graffiti artists.

They formed graffiti groups such as The Fabulous Five, and covered the sides of buildings and subway trains with murals.

WOW! facts
Graffiti goes back much further than hip hop culture. There are examples from Ancient Greece and Rome.

3. The Ages of Rap

Rap has moved through lots of different phases. This is because new artists want to put their own stamp on it rather than simply copying what's gone before.

Here are some different types:

Old school
Artists such as Melle Mel and The Sugarhill Gang scored the first rap hits. Many said the music was just a fad, but it never went away.

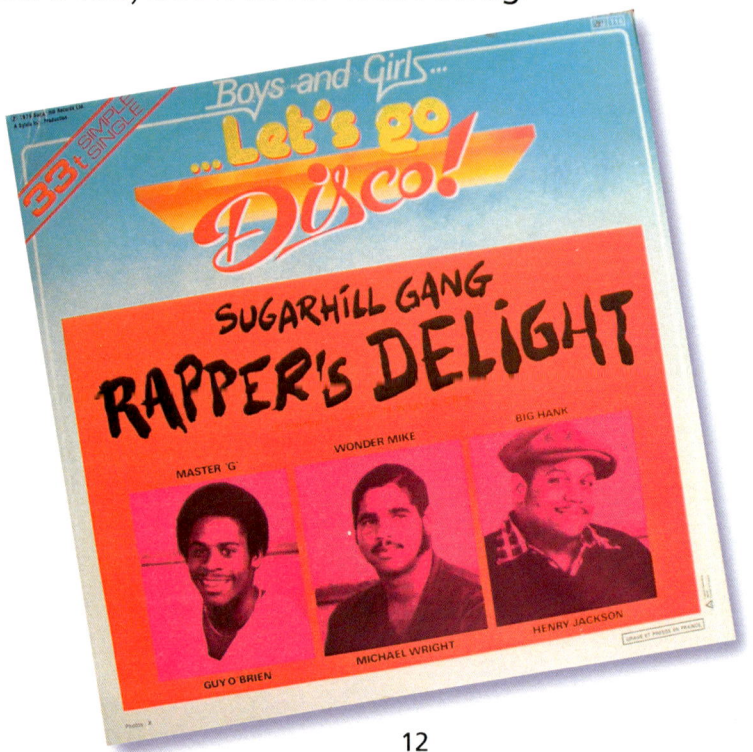

The golden age of rap

Rap was massively successful in the 1980s. Artists such as Run DMC, the Beastie Boys and Public Enemy brought beats and rhymes to new audiences around the world.

Gangsta rap

In the late 1980s, artists such as Ice T rapped about gang life. Some people thought they were encouraging violence.

Tragedy struck gangsta rap in the 1990s when Tupac Shakur and Notorious B.I.G. were both murdered.

Alternative rap

Also in the late 1980s, groups such as De La Soul and A Tribe Called Quest focused on clever lyrics and unusual samples (short snippets taken from other songs).

Rap metal

Bands such as Limp Bizkit and Cyprus Hill crossed rap with heavy metal in the 1990s.

Rap is often mixed with other types of music to create something new.

Pop rap

Pop rap is hip hop music mixed with bits of pop music.

The artist includes catchy choruses in the rap. The choruses are called 'pop hooks'. This has been the most popular form of rap in the 21st century.

People have downloaded the music of artists such as the Black Eyed Peas, the Beastie Boys and Nicki Minaj millions of times.

WOW! facts
In 2014, an American called Aten Williams broke the record for the longest freestyle rap. He made up rap lyrics non-stop for 17 hours.

4. Is rap poetry?

Some people think poetry is something you learn about in school and rap is something you listen to in your spare time. But the two things have a lot in common.

Poets write their poems in different forms, with different rhythms such as ballads or sonnets.

Rappers make their words fit the rhythm of the backing beat.

RAP

- lines often end with rhyming words

e.g.

They say I run the streets

I tell 'em no wonder

The cheapest thang I got on is my belt

And it's $400

(2 Chainz)

POETRY

- lines often end with rhyming words

e.g.

Tyger Tyger, burning bright,

In the forests of the night,

(William Blake)

RAP

- often uses comparisons like similes

e.g.

Coming from the deep black like the Loch Ness

(Talib Kweli)

POETRY

- often uses comparisons like similes

e.g.

I wandered lonely as a cloud

(William Wordsworth)

RAP

- often uses new words

e.g.

Rappers like Snoop Dogg made up lots of words ending '**izzle**' – like '**rizzle dizzle**' meaning 'real deal'.

POETRY

- often uses new words

e.g.

The writer, Lewis Carroll, who wrote Alice in Wonderland invented new words like '**frabjous**' in his poem 'Jabberwocky'.

RAP

- often uses characters e.g.
The rapper, Eminem, wrote from the point of view of a made-up character in his song 'Stan'.

POETRY

- often uses characters e.g.
Some poets such as Robert Browning are known for writing from the point of view of an interesting character.

5. Hip Hop Fashion

Hip hop has inspired many different clothing trends.

The early New York hip hoppers wore sheepskin coats, Clarks shoes and berets. But this look didn't last long.

Fans soon started wearing items such as tracksuits, hooded tops, baseball caps and trainers, and this style has stuck.

In 1985, Run DMC released a track called, 'My Adidas'. The German sportswear brand has been popular in hip hop ever since. Other brands linked with hip hop are Nike, Tommy Hilfiger, DKNY, Gucci, Louis Vuitton and Ecko Unlimited.

Some rappers have created their own fashion brand. In 1995, the Wu-Tang Clan created their Wu Wear label, opening four stores across the USA.

In 1999, Jay Z founded Rocawear, and in 2005, Pharrell Williams launched Billionaire Boys Club.

In the 1990s, the term 'bling' became popular.

It is used for flashy jewellery such as diamond rings and gold chains. It was a way of showing off wealth.

Some thought it was cool, but some thought it was over-the-top and tacky.

Street fashions had a major influence on the catwalk, with brands such as Chanel showing hip hop-themed collections. This was sometimes called 'homeboy chic'.

Hip hop and high fashion are now very closely linked. In 2013, Jay Z even named a track after the designer Tom Ford.

Five classic hip hop fashions:

Adidas trainers with no laces
When Run DMC rapped 'My Adidas', audience members would take their trainers off and hold them in the air.

This would have been quite easy, as it was fashionable at that time to wear trainers without laces.

Kangol Bermuda Casual hat

LL Cool J wore a Kangol Bermuda Casual hat on the cover of his second album, and it became a classic of hip hop fashion. The hat has a bell shape and kangaroo logo.

Harem pants

1990s star, MC Hammer, wore really baggy trousers that got narrow at the ankle. They were influenced by old styles from the Middle East and known as 'harem pants'.

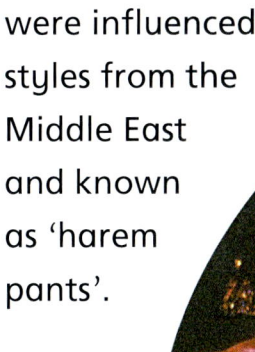

Baseball cap

The baseball cap is a classic part of the hip hop look. Popular designs include the Nike swoosh and the logos of the New York Yankees and Los Angeles Dodgers (baseball teams).

At times it has been fashionable to wear caps backwards or sideways. One fad in the early 2000s was to leave price labels dangling from expensive caps.

The bestselling rappers of all time are Eminem (155 million albums), Jay Z (75 million albums) and Tupac Shakur (75 million albums).

Beats by Dre headphones

Dr. Dre launched his headphone company, Beats, in 2006. They were for hip hop fans who wanted a better-quality bass sound. They came in many different colours and became a popular fashion accessory.

WOW! facts

In 2014, Dr. Dre overtook P Diddy to become the richest rapper in the world. This is because he sold his Beats by Dre headphone business to Apple for three billion dollars.

6. Hip hop around the world

From its early days in New York, hip hop culture spread around the USA and the rest of the world.

Britain was one of the first countries to adopt it. At first, British rap was very similar to American rap, but it soon developed styles of its own. For example:

- **Trip hop** – a form of experimental rap from Bristol.
- **Grime** – a mix of rap and dance music from East London.

Rap soon took off in other languages. Stars included:

- **MC Solaar** – rapped in French.
- **Die Fantastischen Vier** – rapped in German.

Breakdancing also became hugely popular around the world. At the Battle of the Year contest, dancers from countries such as Japan, South Korea, Germany, France, Russia and the USA all compete against each other.

Graffiti inspired by hip hop culture can be seen in many different countries.

There have been several books and exhibitions about British street artist, Banksy. His true identity is still a secret.

WOW! facts

Jay Z never writes his lyrics down. He learns them by heart as he comes up with them.

7. How to Become a Rapper

If reading this book has inspired you to try becoming a rap star yourself, here's what to do.

- Learn your favourite raps off by heart. You can find instrumental versions online to rap along with.

- Record yourself and listen back. How can you improve?

Index

alternative rap 14
Banksy 28
breakdancing 7, 10, 27
DJ 7, 9, 11, 31
Dr. Dre 5, 25
Eminem 5, 18, 24
freestyle rap 15
gangsta rap 13
golden age of rap 13
graffiti 7, 11, 28
grime 26
Jay Z 5, 20, 22, 24, 28
New York 5, 6, 8, 19, 24, 26
old school 12
pop rap 15
rap metal 14
Run DMC 13, 20, 22
toasting 10
trip hop 26
Tupac Shakur 13, 24

7. How to Become a Rapper

If reading this book has inspired you to try becoming a rap star yourself, here's what to do.

- Learn your favourite raps off by heart. You can find instrumental versions online to rap along with.

- Record yourself and listen back. How can you improve?

- Learn to write lyrics. Think about which words rhyme and keep a notebook for ideas. Some rappers can make the words up as they go along, but it takes a lot of practice to get to this level.

- Use music software to create your own beats, or team up with a friend who wants to become a producer.

- When you have a few tracks you're happy with, combine them into a 'mixtape' and release it online.

Questions

Which American city did hip hop start in? (*page 5*)

What are the four elements of hip hop? (*page 7*)

How did the first hip hop DJs create breaks? (*page 9*)

Which clothing label did Run DMC release a track about? (*page 20*)

Who is the bestselling rapper of all time? (*page 24*)

Which city did Grime music come from? (*page 26*)

Index

alternative rap 14
Banksy 28
breakdancing 7, 10, 27
DJ 7, 9, 11, 31
Dr. Dre 5, 25
Eminem 5, 18, 24
freestyle rap 15
gangsta rap 13
golden age of rap 13
graffiti 7, 11, 28
grime 26
Jay Z 5, 20, 22, 24, 28
New York 5, 6, 8, 19, 24, 26
old school 12
pop rap 15
rap metal 14
Run DMC 13, 20, 22
toasting 10
trip hop 26
Tupac Shakur 13, 24